How To Survive An Autopsy

How To Survive An Autopsy

Thomas Brennan

REGENT PRESS
Berekeley, California
2022

Copyright © 2022 by Thomas Brennan

ISBN 13: 978-1-58790-587-2

ISBN 10: 1-58790-587-6

Library of Congress Catalog Number: 2021947824

Manufactured in the U.S.A.
REGENT PRESS
Berkeley, California
www.regentpress.net

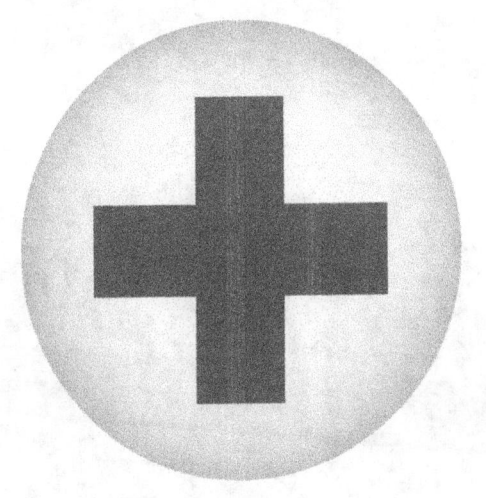

My car is so unsafe to drive — the navigation lady took out extra insurance.

I own a 'leaked' photograph of President Lincoln presiding over a firing squad.

You might be paranoid if you find bird crap on your car and you think it's personal.

Golden Corral – What a strange name for a restaurant. I don't know whether I'm supposed to eat or rope cattle.

You've got to be careful walking around in New York City. One time I put my hand in my pocket – I felt another hand.

I like attending high school reunions. But then again I enjoy drinking brake fluid.

I visited Jimmy Carter recently. He handed me a hammer and some nails and told me to build something.
I left as soon as he informed me about his plans on getting re-elected.

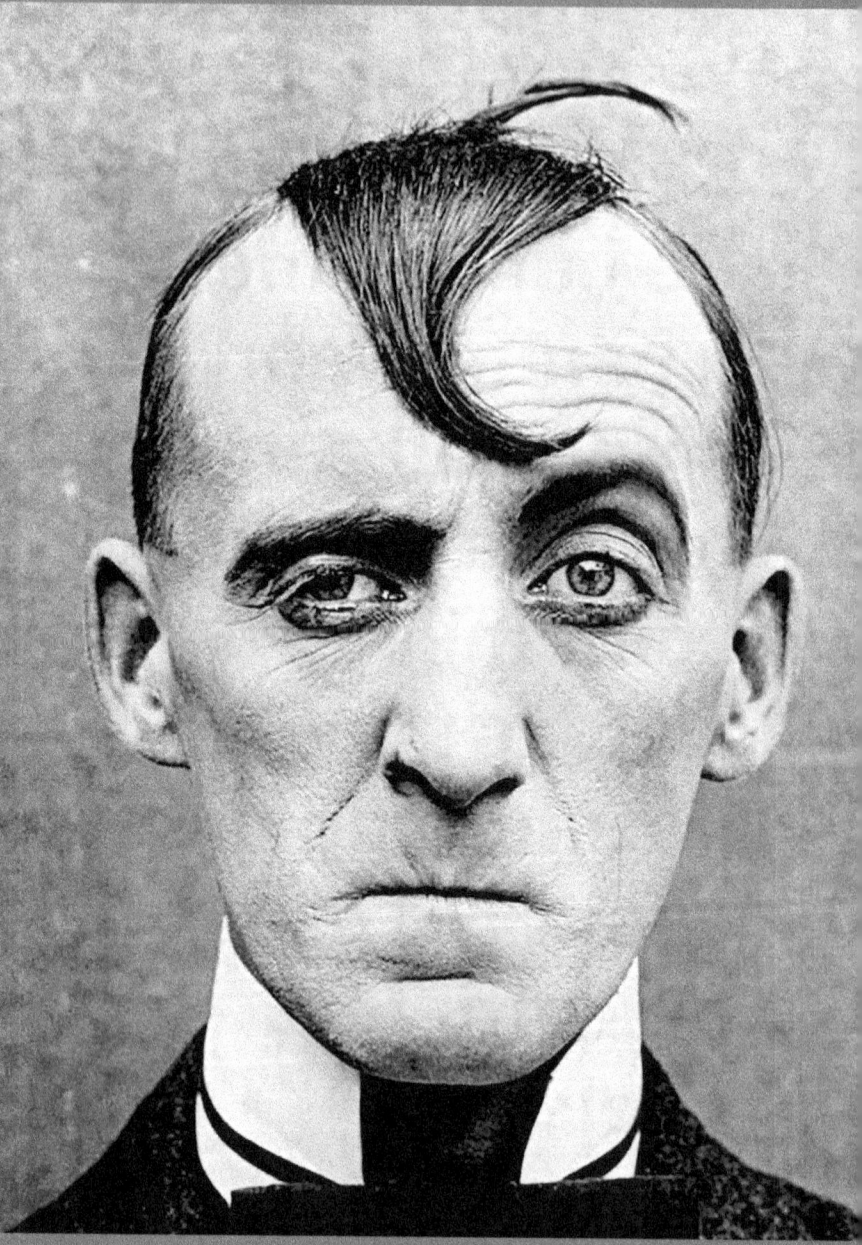

Every neighborhood seems to have at least one weirdo. You know the type. The guy's either got holes with people in them or he's harvesting organs.

How come there's no Channel 1?

My wife doesn't like me walking around in my underwear. Especially when we go out.

Fun fact: The fastest animal in the world is a live chicken at Perdue.

I'm not much of a drinker. One sip of grape juice and I end up in rehab.

My friend is a little high-strung. If the Yankees leave a man on third — he takes hostages.

I'm a little concerned about my friend. His idea of safe sex is when his girlfriend's husband is out of town.

A meat lover's pizza with everything on it is not a meal – it's a cry for help.

My neighbors think I'm anti-social. I don't know – maybe it's the moat.

Stores don't have enough checkout lanes open. The other day I was in line for so long my coupons expired.

I worry about my friend. He thinks mixed nuts are two naked guys dancing.

If God is all powerful then how come He had to rest on the 7th day?

My grandfather was pathologically introverted. For 8 years he pretended to be a bowl of fruit.

My cousin finally got up enough nerve to ask his girlfriend for her hand. He doesn't want to marry her. He just wants her hand.

Living out in the country is not for everyone. Not a whole lot to do. Sometimes I'll sit at home with the missus and watch hunting accidents on TV.

Beverly Hills is so swanky — Taco Bell has strolling violinists.

I never have it easy. One time I kissed the Blarney Stone – I got slapped.

Celery is the only food you can eat and floss with at the same time.

I remember the time I visited Charlton Heston at his home in Idaho. He took me for a ride in his chariot - then he pushed me out to see if I'd bounce.

I have the worst luck. One time I called my mom on Mother's Day. She asked me how I got her number.

I'm not in the best shape. Humming gives me chest pains.

My wife comes from money. I don't want to brag – but the Pope sang at our wedding.

I'm a very impulsive guy. Years ago I moved my family to Utah for the salt.

Good jobs are hard to come by. That's why I don't recommend anyone majoring in Russian art – unless you don't mind ending up as a night manager at Doug's Dildo Emporium.

Has anyone figured out what that tiny pocket on a pair of jeans is for?

I have a pet peeve with people who have pet peeves.

I hate setting my clock back one hour. That means my day's going to suck that much longer.

Every so often I like to watch hockey on TV just to be sure I still hate it.

I wouldn't say I'm dull but when I throw a party the neighbors yell "Louder!"

Confessing your sins makes no sense to me. If God is all-knowing – what's there to confess?

I don't understand why football has a two-minute warning. Notifying me that the game has two minutes to go is not a warning. Telling me there's a lunatic spraying bullets from the 50- yard line – now THAT'S a warning.

Do you want to know what my definition of cheap is? Trying on pants at a yard sale.

I saw a movie that was so horrible - I asked the lady in front of me to put her hat back on.

I spent a week in Kansas once. Big mistake. I called for a ride and a guy showed up in a tractor.

Living in New Jersey can be rough. There's a lot of unsavory characters walking the streets. One bad confrontation and you could end up in someone's deli sandwich.

Online gambling. How convenient. Now you don't have to leave your house to lose your house.

Let's be honest. Gift bags are for people too lazy to wrap.

I'm not very handy around the house. If a light bulb goes out – I figure it's time to move

Philosophy majors are always asking intriguing questions like, "Is that for here or to go?"

WE USE
U.S. GOVERNMENT INSPEC

Old age catches up to most of us. The other day I saw Superman doing a commercial for Miracle-Ear.

I basically have no life. The other day I watched an 8 hour documentary on motel soap.

I remember the first time I pulled a gray hair. My grandfather slapped me.

Facebook users have got to get a life. I'm sorry but your trip to the Waffle House doesn't qualify you as interesting.

When I was growing up there was never enough to eat. It got so bad at one point – the roaches took us to court.

I often wonder when it's too late in the day to say, "Have a nice day."

I'm concerned about my therapist. I told him I'm always on edge. He said not to worry – it's all in my head.

Fun Fact: Creamed corn was first discovered in Iowa when a farmer threw up.

I'm currently working on a non-fiction version of the Bible.

I was with my dear grandfather the day he died. Before he passed away I remember leaning over and whispering in his ear – "Where'd you bury the money?"

I'm all for prison reform. I just don't want somebody on death row getting more channels than me.

We all have our little peculiarities. I like to hide inside a clothes hamper and pretend it's a prison break.

The people at Viagra say you should see your doctor for an erection lasting longer than 4 hours. My question is this. Why ruin a good thing?

Question: What does a man like to hold in his hand more than anything?

Answer: His remote.

You know the romance is over if your partner checks the sports page during sex.

I wouldn't exactly say I'm a square – but cork excites me.

The air quality seems to be getting worse. In fact it's so bad – I was at a funeral and the deceased coughed.

Me and a friend were in a stage production of King Kong – we played his testicles.

I come from a town that's so mean – they named a street after Ted Bundy.

I don't know why they're called speed bumps if you have to slow down.

You probably have a gambling problem if Steve Wynn calls to see how you're doing.

Drivers today are maniacs. My middle finger has seen more action than a hooker at a Shriner's convention.

I went to a circus that was so cheap – only one clown got out of the car.

And what's with those Muppets? Grown adults with their arm up a puppet's keister. C'mon. Find some other line of work. Ever think of welding?

Exchanging vows at the altar was a big moment for me. I was more nervous than a bellhop at the Bates Motel.

I own a rare photograph of the Good Humor Man snorting sprinkles.

Screening at the airport is brutal. My last time there I was patted down, frisked and groped for half an hour – and that's before I got out of the cab.

Am I the only one who thinks of Ned Beatty whenever I hear banjos?

My dog is a little strange. He keeps a picture of my leg over his bowl.

I don't make a very good impression. I was in a store the other day and a lady told me I looked familiar. I said, "Mom – I'm your son."

Stew is soup with an attitude.

I was in Vermont this past winter. There was so much snow – it was whiter than the cast of *Seinfeld*.

**Question:
What does a lion call a tourist on safari?**

**Answer:
Lunch.**

I once had an audience with the Queen. She was so loaded down with jewelry I had to help her back to her throne.

For you single women out there – you should probably dump your man if he has to drop his pants to count to one.

I've had so much work done on my teeth – I have more caps than the New York Yankees.

I don't know why Jesus is sometimes depicted as having blond hair and blue eyes. He was a Middle Eastern – not a Viking.

My dog worships me. It figures. The only one who looks up to me drinks out of a toilet.

Fun fact: It has recently been confirmed by biblical scholars that at The Last Supper nobody picked up the check.

Big cities are experiencing so many shootings – joggers are running serpentine.

General Custer's last words at Little Big Horn: "We got this."

You might want to rethink your career path if your sofa has more change in it than your bank account.

Going hunting with my dad was always a big thrill. He'd slap some antlers on me and tell me to start running.

Have you noticed the tinier the dog — the wealthier the person is holding it?

When you think about it – isn't Cousin It the first example of gender fluidity?

Have you ever noticed every bald, white guy looks like Lex Luthor?

When you call out sick from work - does a part of you think your boss doesn't believe you?

I know what a kit is – but what the hell is a caboodle?

The potholes in New York City are so huge – I saw one that had its own Starbucks.

Fun Fact: Making eye contact in an elevator is considered 'aggressive behavior' in Cleveland.

How come we're friendlier with a dog than we are with the person walking it?

If there's a West Virginia – how come there's not an East Virginia?

Gasoline is so expensive – I saw a getaway driver pushing his car.

I worry about guys who propose during a lap dance.

You can tell you're possessed if you reach for something and it's not your hand.

I've read that Botox users can't move their facial muscles. Their expression's the same whether they're having an orgasm or cooking an omelet.

If you still use a fold-up map to get around – you need to be displayed in a museum.

You're probably up there in years if you leave a swingers party early just to beat the traffic.

Airlines have got to stop cramming people together. Take my last flight. I sat so close to the lady in front of me – we're now expecting twins.

Why is it every time someone dies unexpectedly they're always described by everyone as having been warm and loveable? I guess Hell must be empty.

Baseball is the kind of game where you can slip into a coma and not miss a play.

My uncle finally found the love of his life. Unfortunately he has to keep putting air in it.

My parents were a little odd. They made me and my brother play cops and robbers with real bullets.

It seems everyone is stressed out these days. Last week my anger management coach took a swing at me.

I own a rare photograph of Smokey the Bear attacking a campsite.

Pet Peeve: When the directions on my diet medication say I need to take it with food.

Global warming is getting worse. The other day I saw the Statue of Liberty skinning dipping in the East River.

**Idea for a new state license plate:
Iowa – We have the best hoes.**

Fun Fact: In the state of Michigan you can get 10 years for forging your own signature.

You can tell the romance is over if you and your date arrive at a club and she tells you to wait outside.

Never trust anyone who can't say 'moist' without grinning.

The years go by so quickly. Before you know it you're sitting in a rest home with your teeth in a jar waiting for a stone to pass.

Wanna have some fun? The next time you're at a restaurant – ask a family if they wouldn't mind you joining them.

Jeff Bezos' house is so huge – it has its own weather.

**That's
all
for
the
moment
folks
. . .**

www.ingramcontent.com/pod-product-compliance
Lightning Source LLC
Chambersburg PA
CBHW070107080526
44586CB00013B/1215

9781587905872